This book belongs to

Ce livre appartient à

To parents and teachers

We hope this book will be fun to use in either English or French. Here are a few helpful tips:

- When you start learning a foreign language, it's very useful to learn words that are similar to your own language, like the words in this book.
- Although the words and letters look very similar in French and English, they are not usually *spoken* the same way. Have fun pronouncing the foreign language with your child.
- Don't worry if your pronunciation isn't quite right. The pronunciation guide will help, but it cannot be completely accurate. You should read it as naturally as possible, but don't roll the r. Put stress on the letters in *italics,* for example, lambool-*anss*. Ask a French-speaking person to help you if you can.
- Encourage the children to try and then give them lots of praise. Little children are usually quite un-self-conscious, and this is excellent for building up confidence in a foreign language.
- Use the full alphabet at the top of the page to teach the alphabetica order. Try saying the whole alphabet in English and French, and answer the quiz questions at the end of the book.

First edition for the United States, its Dependencies, Canada, and the Philippines published in 2009
by Barron's Educational Series, Inc., Hauppauge, NY, USA.

Address all inquiries to:
Barron's Educational Series, Inc.
250 Wireless Boulevard
Hauppauge, NY 11788
www.barronseduc.com

ISBN-13: 978-0-7641-4262-8
ISBN-10: 0-7641-4262-3

Library of Congress Control Number: 2008933960

Printed in China
9 8 7 6 5 4 3 2 1

Alphabet

L'alphabet

lalfa-*beh*

Catherine Bruzzone

Illustrations by Louise Comfort
Illustré par Louise Comfort

BARRON'S

[redacted]

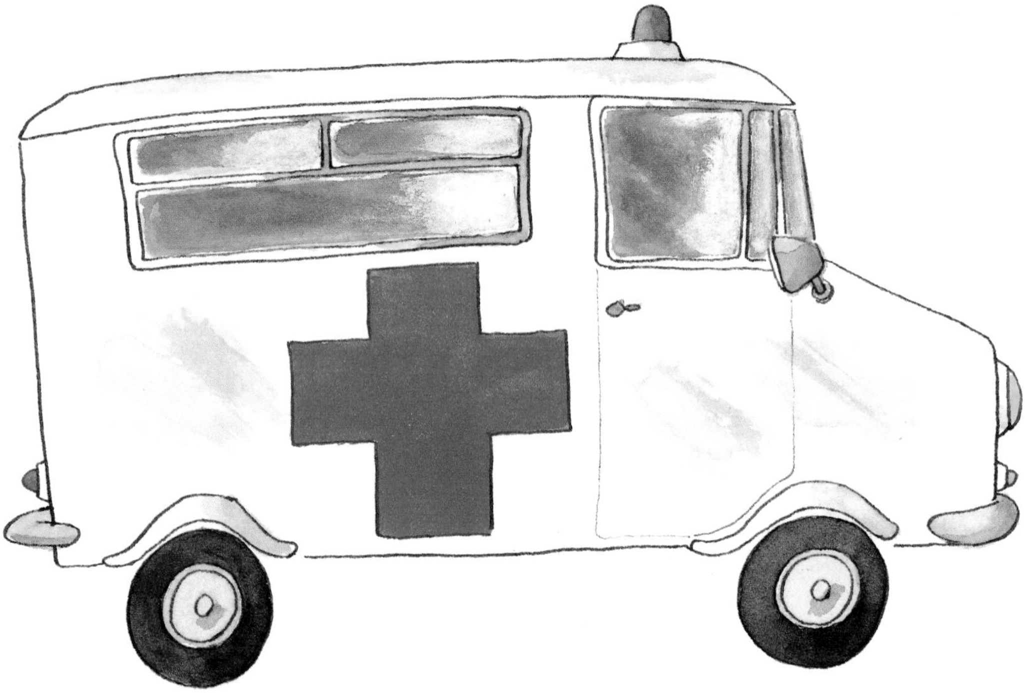

Aa

ambulance
l'ambulance

ah

lambool-*anss*

Bb

ball

la balle

beh

lah bal

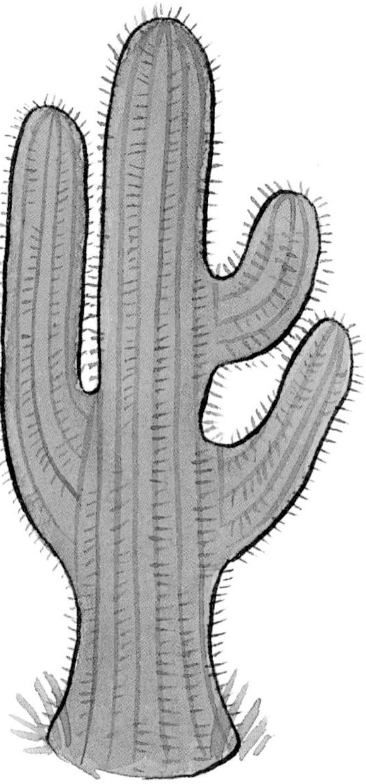

Cc

cactus

le cactus

seh

leh kak-*toos*

Dd

dolphin
le dauphin

deh

leh doh-*fahn*

Ee

elephant
l'éléphant

eh lel-lay-*fahn*

Ff

fire

le feu

eff leh feh

Gg

gorilla
le gorille

shay

leh gor-*eel*

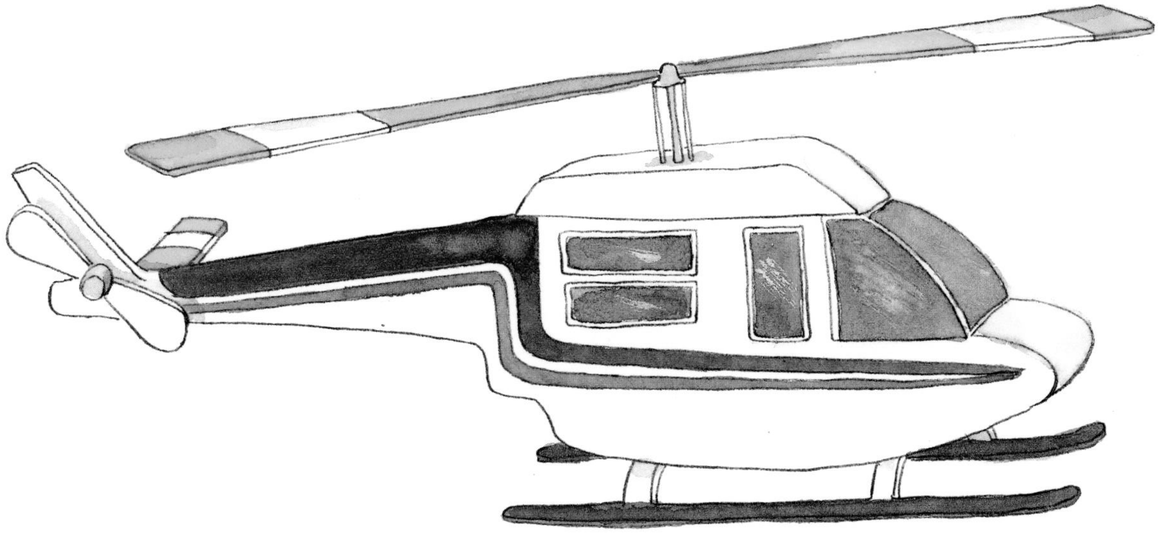

Hh

helicopter

l'hélicoptère

ash

lel-li-cop-*tair*

Ii

igloo
l'igloo

ee

lig-*loo*

Jj

jungle
la jungle

shee lah shun-gl'

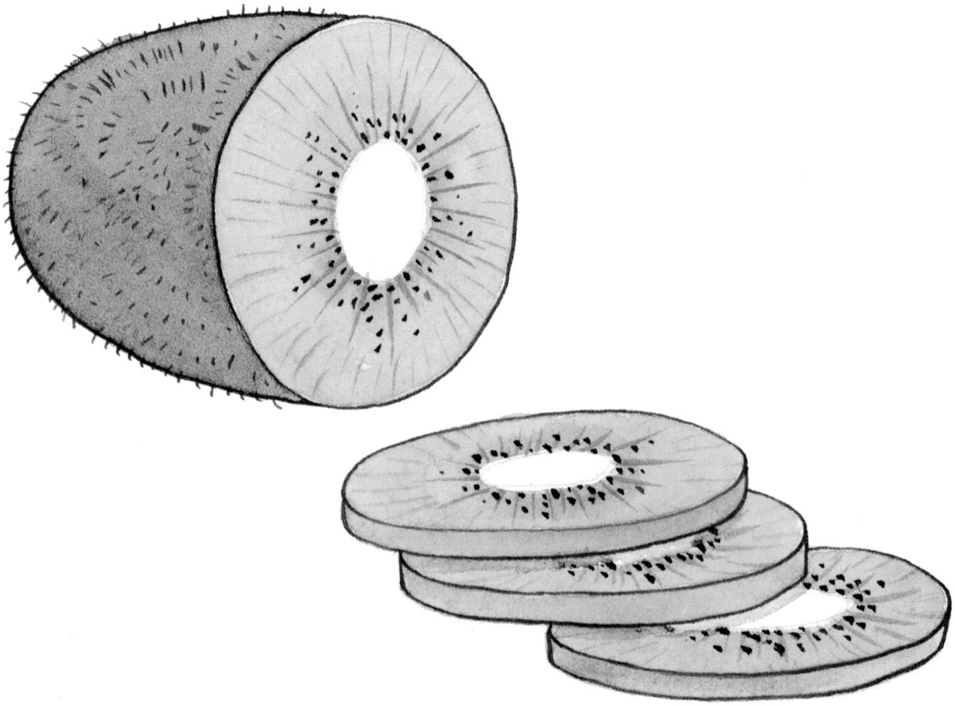

Kk

kiwi

le kiwi

kah

leh kee-*wee*

Ll

lion

le lion

ell

leh lee-*yohn*

Mm

mountain
la montagne

em

lah mon-*tyne*

Nn **night** la nuit

en

lah nwee

Oo

ogre

l'ogre

oh loh-gr'

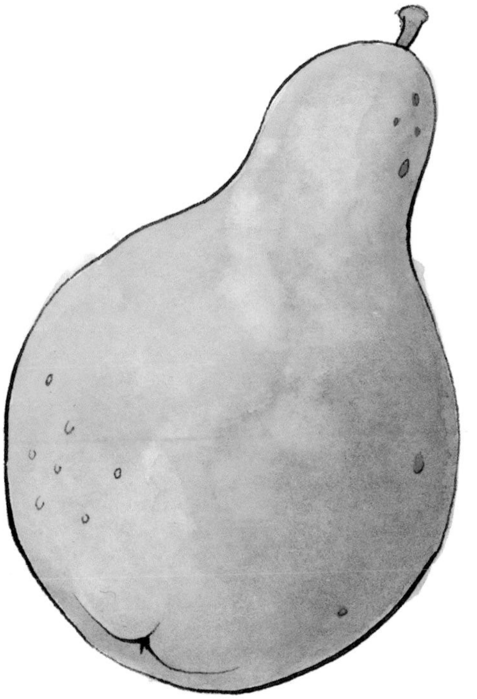

Pp

pear

la poire

peh lah pwahr

Qq

quintuplets
les quintuplées

koo

leh kan-too-*pleh*

Rr

reindeer

le renne

air leh ren

Ss

sun
le soleil

ess

leh sol-*ay*

Tt

tomato

la tomate

teh

lah toh-*mat*

Uu

universe

l'univers

oo

loony-*vair*

Vv

violin

le violon

veh

leh vee-o-*lohn*

Ww

wok

le wok

doubl' *veh*

leh wok

Xx

xylophone

le xylophone

eeks

leh kseelo-*fon*

Yy

yacht

le yacht

ee-*grek*

leh yot

Zz

zoo

le zoo

zed

leh zooh

The End

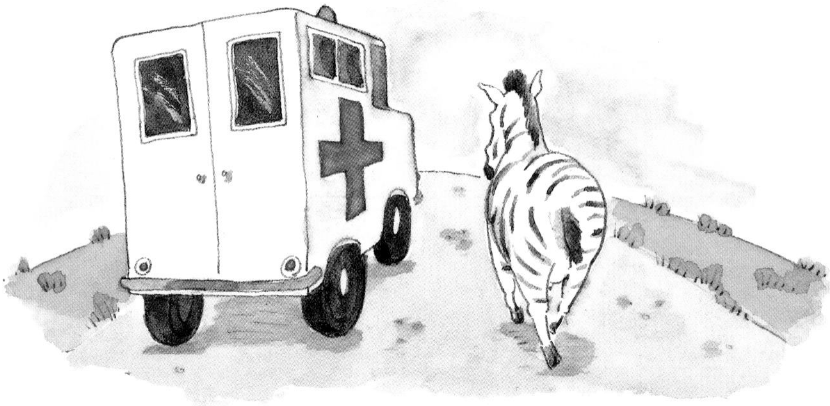

Fin

fahn

ABC QUIZ

Read these aloud in French, in the ***correct*** alphabetical order.

 la **b**alle

 l'**a**mbulance

 le **c**actus

 l'**h**élicoptère

 l'**i**gloo

 le **g**orille

Can you say the names for the following pictures in French?
Now say them in alphabetical order.

j  v  d 

l  s 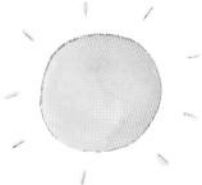 n 

p  m  t 

b c d e g i k m

What are the missing letters?
Say them out loud in French. Now say the whole alphabet.

n o s t u w y z

Check the answers by looking back through the book.